A Kid's Guide to Drawing™

How to Draw Cartoon Careers

Curt Visca and Kelley Visca

The Rosen Publishing Group's
PowerKids Press™
New York

Dedicated to Kelley's parents, Ken and Alrene, who have
encouraged her in her teaching and writing careers

Published in 2004 by The Rosen Publishing Group, Inc.
29 East 21st Street, New York, NY 10010

First Edition

Editor: Natashya Wilson
Book Design: Kim Sonsky
Layout Design: Michael J. Caroleo

Illustration Credits: All illustrations © Curt Visca.
Photo Credits: Cover and p. 14 © Bruce Burkhardt/CORBIS; p. 6 © Layne Kennedy/CORBIS; p. 8 © Richard Hutchings/CORBIS; p. 10 © Skjold Photographs; p. 12 © Jose Luis Peleaz Inc./CORBIS; pp. 16, 20 © Owen Franken/CORBIS; p. 18 © Peter Morgan/Reuters/TIMEPIX.

Visca, Curt.
How to draw cartoon careers / Curt Visca and Kelley Visca.— 1st ed.
    p. cm. — (A kid's guide to drawing)
Summary: Provides facts about different kinds of careers and step-by-step instructions for drawing cartoon representatives of each one, including a fireman, a chef, and a farmer.
Includes bibliographical references and index.
ISBN 0-8239-6725-5 (lib. bdg.)
1. Occupations in art—Juvenile literature. 2. Cartooning—Technique—Juvenile literature. [1. Occupations in art. 2. Cartooning—Technique. 3. Drawing—Technique.] I. Visca, Kelley. II. Title. III. Series.
NC825.O3 V57 2004
741.5—dc21

                         2002008654

Manufactured in the United States of America

CONTENTS

1	Cartoon Careers	4
2	Firefighters	6
3	Police Officers	8
4	Teachers	10
5	Doctors	12
6	Construction Workers	14
7	Chefs	16
8	Mail Carriers	18
9	Farmers	20
	Terms for Drawing Cartoons	22
	Glossary	23
	Index	24
	Web Sites	24

Cartoon Careers

Have you ever thought about which job or career you would like to have when you grow up? Maybe you would like to be a construction worker and build **skyscrapers**. Perhaps you would like to be a teacher and help children to learn.

More than 125 million people are working today in the United States. There are many different careers from which to choose! You may decide to work in an office, in a store, in a factory, outdoors, or even at home. The job you choose may **require** you to go to college or to a trade school to learn special skills and earn a **degree** or a **credential**.

This book will teach you about eight careers and how to draw a cartoon person doing each job. Reading this book and drawing the cartoons might help you to decide what you would like to do when you grow up!

Cartoon people at work are a lot of fun to draw. You will only include the most important lines and shapes to keep your drawings simple. If your cartoon people look different from the ones in the book, that's great! Just as everyone looks different, everyone draws differently, too. As a cartoonist, you will develop your own cartooning style, or way of drawing. Your style will make your drawings special.

You will need the following supplies to draw cartoon careers:

- Paper
- A sharp pencil or a felt-tipped marker
- An eraser
- Colored pencils or crayons to add color

When you draw your cartoons, sit at a desk or a table in a quiet place. Make sure that there is plenty of light and that you have all your supplies handy. Directions underneath the drawing steps will help you to add each new part of your cartoon. New parts are shown in red. The Terms for Drawing Cartoons list on page 22 names and shows many of the drawing shapes.

Remember to take your time, to try your best, and to practice your cartoons over and over again. It won't be long before you become a creative cartoonist!

A firefighter, a doctor, a chef, let's see. What might be the best job for me?

Firefighters

Firefighters rush to fires to help people and to put out the flames. Their first job is to free anyone who is trapped. They help people who are injured. Firefighters also teach people about fire **prevention**. In the 1600s in North America, firefighters were called bucket brigades. Townspeople formed lines from a fire to a well and passed buckets of water to the fire. Today firefighters arrive at a fire in several vehicles. The fire engine carries water and hoses. The ladder truck has ladders that reach up to 100 feet (30 m) high. The rescue truck carries tools that are used to break through walls and metal to reach people who are trapped. Firefighters wear special clothes and helmets to protect themselves from fire. They carry air tanks on their backs. To become a firefighter, you must pass **physical** and written tests. Physical tests can include carrying heavy fire hoses and ladders over **obstacles**.

Let's make a long, thin, wavy oval shape for the brim of the helmet. Draw three straight lines for the front plate. Finish the top of the helmet by making three curved lines.

2

Draw a short line below the helmet, then a circle and a letter C. Add dots inside. Make a letter C for the nose and letter U's for the mustache. Add a curved line. Make a mouth.

3

From the helmet to the chin, make two long straight lines and a short line. Make some hair. Draw a curved line with a line inside for the ear. Add a curved line to finish the head.

4

Make two bent lines for the sleeve. Add a rectangle for the cuff. Start the hand with a short straight line. Add a curved line for the thumb. Make three letter U's for fingers.

5

Make a rectangle, angled lines, and a letter C for the hose's tip. Add a dot inside. Draw curved lines for fingers. Add two lines for the hose, and two lines to finish the coat.

6

Add water, fire, and action lines. Draw lines and ovals to complete the jacket. Decorate the helmet.

7

Police Officers

There are about 740,000 police officers serving in the United States. They make sure that laws are obeyed. Police officers protect people and property in communities. They direct traffic, find people who are lost, and help people to settle fights. They also **patrol**

streets to prevent crime and to keep people safe.

Sometimes police officers are called cops. This might be because the initials "c.o.p." stood for "**constable** on patrol" in the 1800s. One story says that "cop" is short for the copper badges that the first New York police officers wore in the 1840s. Another says it comes from "cop," meaning to catch or nab.

To become a police officer, you must attend a police school. As a **recruit**, you learn about laws, weapons, and other subjects. You train with another officer and ride along on calls in his or her police car.

Start with a star. Draw curved lines around it for the hat. Make two letter *U*'s and two bent lines for sunglasses. Add curved lines for the ear and head. Make hair using straight lines.

Draw a long nose. Add a line, then curved lines for lips. Make two curved lines for the head and a letter *U* for the neck. Make a whistle on a string using curved lines.

Next draw the shirt, using straight lines. Make the belt and club using squares, an oval, and straight lines. Draw triangles for a collar. Add shoulder patches and a star badge.

You did it! Make the hands and fingers using curved lines and ovals. Draw an octagon with a smaller one inside it for the stop sign. Add straight lines to make the handle.

Make two straight lines and an upside-down letter *U* for the pants. Draw three straight lines and two slightly curved lines for each boot.

Draw straight lines for the crosswalk. Add detail to your officer. Add action lines. Write "STOP."

Teachers

Nearly 50 million men and women throughout the world are teachers. This is more people than are in any other career. To be a teacher, you have to go to college and earn a degree. Then you continue with a teacher training program to earn your teaching credential. To teach kindergarten through sixth grade, you need training in multiple subjects, including math, reading, and science. To teach junior high and high school, you would specialize in a single subject, such as math. To teach in college, you need at least a master's degree.

In the 1800s, schoolhouses had just one room. One teacher taught up to 60 children in all different grade levels, from first through eighth grade. Students studied reading, writing, history, geography, and math, much as they do today. Today most public schools have from 20 to 35 students in each room.

Begin your teacher by making a big, upside-down *U*. Add straight lines and upside-down letter *V*'s for the hair. Draw a letter *U* for the chin.

2

Draw two circles with dots inside for the eyes. Make eyelashes. Add a letter *C* for the nose. Make a straight line and a letter *U* for the mouth. Add teeth and a tongue, then shade.

3

A+! Make a letter *U* for the neck. Add two curved lines for the collar. Draw a curved line and a straight line for each shoulder. Add detail on the sleeves.

4

Start by the sleeves and draw two bent lines down the sides. Add a slightly curved line at the bottom to finish the dress. Make a bumpy line at the bottom of the dress.

5

Draw bent lines for the arms. On the left, add a rectangle for a watch. Draw curved lines for the thumbs and fingers. Add chalk and paper. Draw straight lines for the legs.

6

Add details, such as a desk and a chalkboard. Write a class list and a test. Make up a caption.

LIBRARY

11

Doctors

Medical doctors are people who **diagnose diseases** and wounds, help to treat people who are sick, and give advice on how to stay healthy. About 11.5 million people in the United States work in healthcare. Nearly 800,000 of them are doctors. To become a doctor, you must be a really good student. You must learn many different types of science. Becoming a doctor takes about 11 years of study after high school.

There are many different fields, or areas, of medicine that doctors specialize in and that require special knowledge. For example, **pediatricians** work with children. **Ophthalmologists** treat illnesses of the eyes. **Cardiologists** treat heart problems. To work with families, a doctor specializes in family practice. Doctors become **experts** in their chosen fields!

1

Draw two circles for the headlamp. Make a rectangle for the band. Add lines for the top of the head. For hair, make four bent lines and a line at the top. Make a *U* for the chin.

2

Draw ovals and dots for the eyes. Make eyelashes and the nose. Make a mouth with a tongue and shade it. Draw a thin letter *U* for the neck and two triangles for the collar.

3

Next draw three slightly bent lines for the coat. Make a line down the middle, and add dots for buttons. Add a square for a name tag. Draw a pocket with a pen in it.

4

Start the arms with slightly curved lines. On the left, draw straight lines and detail for a clipboard. Add two ovals for fingers. Draw three straight lines for the other arm.

5

Draw a cuff. Add two lines for the wrist and a curved line for the thumb. Make three ovals for fingers. Draw straight lines to make the needle. Add the pants and shading.

6

Use different lines and shapes to draw a patient on a bed. Add action lines and a caption.

Construction Workers

If you like to build things, a job in construction might be for you. There are more than seven million construction workers in the United States today.

Many parts of a construction worker's job require strength. The work includes carrying building materials, digging **trenches**, and mixing and pouring concrete. Construction workers use tools such as jackhammers, drills, saws, and cranes. Many construction workers specialize in skilled trades, such as carpentry, painting, plumbing, and electrical work.

The first buildings were made of sticks, mud, and rocks. In the 1600s, 20,000 construction workers built the Taj Mahal complex in India in 22 years. Today buildings are made from steel, concrete, glass, and wood. Skyscrapers can be built within two years. The Petronas Towers, the world's tallest buildings at 1,483 feet (452 m) high, took four years to build.

1

Make a bell shape for the hard hat. Draw two small lines to start the head. Make curved lines with smaller lines inside for the ears. Draw a letter *U* for the face. Shade in some hair.

2

Perfect! Make two circles for eyes and two shaded circles inside for pupils. Draw a curved line for the nose. Add a straight line and a curved line for the mouth, and shade.

3

Make a curved line and two straight lines for each sleeve. Draw two straight lines for each arm. Make straight lines and letter *U*'s for gloves. Draw sideways letter *V*'s on each side.

4

Great work! Make straight lines for the top of the jackhammer. Add two squares and a rectangle to complete this section.

5

Make straight lines for each leg. Draw four lines for each boot. Add three letter *U*'s on each boot to show shoelaces.

6

Add detail and action lines. Draw rectangle shapes with squares inside for buildings. Dynamite!

15

Chefs

Whenever you eat at a restaurant, your food is made by a chef or a cook. A chef is usually someone with more experience and skills than a cook. Some chefs learn their skills by going to special **culinary** schools. Others learn on the job, by working as cooks for experienced chefs. It can take from 8 to 15 years to become a chef. Chefs and cooks measure, mix, and cook **ingredients** by following a **recipe**. They use many different pots, pans, ovens, grills, blenders, **cutlery**, and other kitchen equipment.

Chefs cook food in different ways. They bake it in an oven, fry it in oil or butter, boil it in water, grill it, or steam it. Restaurant chefs prepare meals that have been ordered from a restaurant's menu. Often they plan the menu. Some chefs become famous for their own special recipes. Some chefs have their own TV shows! Julia Child and Wolfgang Puck are two famous chefs who have appeared on television.

1

Let's begin by making two connected curved lines for the top of the chef's hat. Draw three straight lines to complete it. Make curved lines for the hair. Shade it in.

2

Start the head with two lines. Add curved lines for ears. Make a letter *U* for the jaw. Draw eyes with big pupils. Add a letter *U* for the nose. Make the mustache and the mouth.

3

Sensational! Make two ovals, a small circle, and two more ovals for a scarf. Draw straight lines and two slightly bent lines for the apron.

4

Next draw three straight lines for each sleeve. Make two straight lines for each arm. Draw a curved line for each thumb and three ovals for fingers on each side.

5

Beautiful! Make straight lines for the spatula. Add two rectangles inside it. Make a letter *U* and two straight lines for the spoon handle. Add an oval and a curved line for the top.

6

Draw bowls of food, a tray, salt, a spoon, a table, and a caption. Add action lines and detail.

17

Mail Carriers

Mail carriers deliver more than 170 billion pieces of mail per year. To become a mail carrier, you must take a special postal exam. The exam includes questions about finding numbers in a series, checking addresses, and memorizing addresses.

Do you ever wonder what happens when you mail a letter? After you put a letter in your mailbox, a mail carrier picks it up and takes it to a sorting center at the post office. It is sent through a machine that places a **cancellation mark** on the stamp. The machine prints a **postmark** and a **barcode** on the envelope. The barcode matches the zip code. Another machine reads the barcode and puts the letter with other letters that are addressed to the same zip code. The letters go by plane or truck to the city that matches that zip code. The letters are sorted again when they arrive. A mail carrier picks up your letter along with other mail and delivers it to the address on the envelope.

1

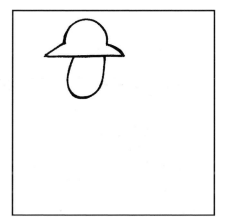

Start by making a long straight line, two short lines, and a curved line for the hat. Draw a letter *U* for the head.

4

Draw two bent lines for each arm. Make curved lines for the thumbs. Add rectangles for letters and a bent line inside the letter on the right.

2

Draw two curved lines on each side for hair. Make two circles for eyes. Add dots. Draw a curved line for the nose. Make two letter *U*'s for the mouth. Add a tongue, and shade.

5

You are first class! Make a large square for the mailbag. Add straight lines for more letters. Add slightly bent lines for the pants. Don't forget the stripes!

3

Draw lines for the neck and triangles for the collar. Add a scarf. Make a long, thin rectangle for a bag strap. Draw curved lines and straight lines for the sleeves and body.

6

Write "MAIL" on the hat and the bag. Add detail, action lines, and a caption. Draw a mailbox.

Farmers

Farmers have some of the most important jobs in the world. They grow crops and raise animals for people to eat. There are about three million farmers working on more than two million farms

in the United States. To become a farmer, you can attend an **agricultural** college to learn about different kinds of farming. There you will learn how to run a business and operate farming machines.

There are many different kinds of farms. On crop farms, farmers grow grains, fruits, and vegetables. Dairy farmers raise cows for milking. **Poultry** farmers raise chickens and turkeys for eggs and meat. Cattle, hog, and sheep farmers raise animals for meat.

Farmers use many special machines. On a crop farm, a tractor is used to move other machines, such as a plow, a **cultivator**, and a seed drill. The plow's thick blades break up hard soil. The cultivator smooths the soil. Then the seed drill plants seeds for the crop.

1

Make a thin, curved shape for the hat brim. Add two curved lines on top. Draw a line for the forehead. Make the eyes. Add a letter C for the nose.

2

Make a bumpy line for the mustache. Add a curved line under it. Draw the mouth, and shade it in. Add a letter C and a line for the ear. Make bumpy lines for the beard and hair.

3

Make the top of the farmer's overalls from straight lines. Add a short line on the front of the shirt. Draw straight lines to make the sleeves and rectangles to make the cuffs.

4

Make straight lines for the wrists and curved lines for the fingers. Draw a long, thin letter U for the pitchfork handle. Add curved lines and two letter V's for the pitchfork.

5

Super work! Finish the overalls by drawing straight lines to make the sides and pant legs. Make the boots from straight and curved lines. Add some shading.

6

Draw detail on the farmer. Make a house, a barn, trees, and chicks. Add action lines. Nice job!

21

Terms for Drawing Cartoons

Here are some of the words and shapes that you need to know to draw cartoon careers:

((	Action lines	V	Letter V
ʔ	Bent lines	⬡	Octagon
Ɛ w	Bumpy Line	⬭	Oval
🗨	Caption	▭	Rectangle
○	Circle	⬛	Shading
⌒	Curved line	☐	Square
Ɛ ⋮⋮ ⌣⌣	Detail	☆	Star
∴	Dots	☰	Straight lines
C	Letter C	△	Triangle
U	Letter U		

Glossary

agricultural (a-grih-KUL-chuh-rul) Having to do with farms and farming.

barcode (BAR-kohd) Printed lines and spaces that are read by computers to label an item.

cancellation mark (kan-suh-LAY-shun MARK) Wavy lines placed over a stamp on a letter so that it cannot be reused.

cardiologists (kar-dee-AH-luh-jists) Doctors who treat people's hearts.

constable (KON-stuh-bul) A minor court officer, sometimes the equal of a policeman.

credential (krih-DEN-shul) A title earned by learning certain skills.

culinary (KUH-lih-neh-ree) Having to do with cooking.

cultivator (KUL-tih-vayt-er) A machine that loosens soil for planting crops.

cutlery (KUT-luh-ree) Knives, spoons, forks, and other eating tools.

degree (duh-GREE) A title given to a person who has finished a course of study.

diagnose (dy-ig-NOHS) To figure out problems by looking at the signs.

diseases (duh-ZEEZ-ez) Illnesses or sicknesses.

experts (EK-sperts) People who know a lot about a subject.

ingredients (in-GREE-dee-unts) Parts of a mixture.

obstacles (OB-stih-kulz) Things that are in the way.

ophthalmologists (of-thuh-MAH-luh-jists) Doctors who treat people's eyes.

patrol (puh-TROHL) To walk or drive around an area to keep it safe.

pediatricians (pee-dee-uh-TRIH-shunz) Doctors who treat children.

physical (FIH-zih-kul) Having to do with the body.

postmark (POHST-mark) A mark that shows when and from where a letter was mailed.

poultry (POHL-tree) Birds, such as chickens, raised for their meat or eggs.

prevention (prih-VEN-shun) Keeping something from happening.

recipe (REH-suh-pee) A set of directions for making something.

recruit (ree-KROOT) A new member of a group.

require (rih-KWYR) To make something necessary.

skyscrapers (SKY-skray-perz) Very tall buildings.

trenches (TRENCH-ez) Long pits dug into the ground.

Index

A
agricultural college, 20
animals, 20

B
barcode, 18
bucket brigades, 6

C
chef(s), 5, 16
Child, Julia, 16
college, 4, 10
construction, 4, 14
cook(s), 16
credential, 4, 10
crops, 20
culinary schools, 16
cultivator, 20

D
degree, 4, 10
diseases, 12
doctor(s), 5, 12

F
farmers, 20
firefighter(s), 5–6

H
healthcare, 12

L
letter(s), 18

M
mail carriers, 18
master's degree, 10

P
pediatricians, 12
Petronas Towers, 14
plow, 20
police officers, 8
postmark, 18
post office, 18
Puck, Wolfgang, 16

R
recruit, 8

S
schoolhouses, 10
science, 12
seed drill, 20
skyscrapers, 4, 14

T
Taj Mahal, 14
teacher(s), 4, 10
tools, 14
tractor, 20

Z
zip code, 18

Web Sites

Due to the changing nature of Internet links, PowerKids Press has created an online list of Web sites related to the subject of this book. This site is updated regularly. Please use this link to access the list: www.powerkidslinks.com/kgd/careers/